REIGN OF THE
QUISLING-RODENTS

NGOLLE-METUGE

Langaa Research & Publishing CIG
Mankon, Bamenda

Publisher:
Langaa RPCIG
Langaa Research & Publishing Common Initiative Group
P.O. Box 902 Mankon
Bamenda
North West Region
Cameroon
Langaagrp@gmail.com
www.langaa-rpcig.net

Distributed outside N. America by African Books Collective
orders@africanbookscollective.com
www.africanbookcollective.com

Distributed in N. America by Michigan State University Press
msupress@msu.edu
www.msupress.msu.edu

ISBN: 9956-578-02-9

DISCLAIMER
All views expressed in this publication are those of the author and do
not necessarily reflect the views of Langaa RPCIG.

DEDICATION

For Mama Mary ETIH and every fatherland's orphans of state; That suffering ends though remembrance never does.

Also for Enongene Kang Andrew, Delphine and Leonie Metuge, Taku Victor Jong and a man named Oben Douglas Otu.

TABLE OF CONTENT

II/NINETEEN BUGLE CALLS 37

INTRODUCTION

Reign of the Quisling-Rodents is, at once, a lament and a call to resistance couched in modern prose-poetry. It is a volume in two parts; the first entitled "Treasons of Malversation" seeks to uncover a society at the brink of socio-economic auto-annihilation through the nefarious human phenomena of egoism and corruption. The quintessence of the work is seen in the utter dehumanization undergone by both the victim of this phenomena represented by the persona in the various poems, and the perpetrator, represented by the unnamed, implied human forces behind these ills suffered by the victim. These unnamed, implied human forces are the

"…pairs and pairs
Of black hands that throw a shroud
Over the sun" (see **ABYSS**)

They both thus become dehumanized in the sense that while the victim is reduced to sub-human status by dint of the privation and destitution he is seen going through in the various poems, the perpetrator, on his part, is imbued with animal qualities by virtue of his capability to transcend the frontiers of human nature in his unleashing of such extreme tribulations to his victims.

The outcome of corruption suffered by the persona in the poems is a function of the unspeakable rapacity that has ravaged the mindset of the society in question. That is to say the constant recurrence of the deprivation motif in almost every stanza of each poem in the volume is testimony to the hypothesis that it is the entire collective consciousness of the society that has been perverted or destroyed by the ills decried. The poet puts his reader in a situation where these ills and their resultant devastation are seen in the pathos-ridden, anguish-filled lines and stanzas.

The volume owes its title from acts, in wanton terribleness, of kleptomania in high places which has held the society sway, pointing to a betrayal of that society, in the Quisling fashion, by its leaders. This kleptomania which has so ravaged the society can be paralleled to the destruction wrought by the pilfering of rodents.

The volume's second part, "Nineteen Bugle Calls", constitutes a refusal to be resigned to the society's dire fate. Here, the poet incorporates into each lament a battle call to resistance against these damnable phenomena in the society; a resistance which must be staged in literary as well as other circles.

N.M

I

TREASONS OF MALVERSATION

IDENTITY

Oil of penury
In a frying-pan country
In it I sizzle
To a crisp delicacy
For fanged, cannibalistic mouths

The noontide blaze
Heats up privation's branding iron;
A red-hot misery
Scars me to the soul

My identity, O! Friend,
Is not the black-hide sticker you see;
This peel*able* label I carry about on me.
It is that indelibleness
Of tribulation
Embossed
On my very essence

ABYSS

My suffering consists
Of two red-coloured woes,
Ten thousand brown pains
And a gripe
Of hunger;
Rumble of thunder
Down in my bowels

Pus –like milk – of human vileness

Flows through a people's veins
To collect in ulcerous mind-breasts,
The addled nipples of which
I suckle from
To drift
Into this nightmare,
Lain
In the in-spiked cradle
Of our forefathers

My kind of suffering I say
Is made up
Of crucifixion nails
Driven
Past the body
Into the soul,
Of unnameable goings on
Behind the black-suit curtains;
Devilry in shadowed nooks
And of pairs and pairs
Of black hands that throw a shroud
Over the sun

Nsokika*
You of all men
I drench in these emerald tears;
Saint whose breath of jasmine
Deodorizes my home
Fouled
By the reek of cupidity-farts

* Bernard Fonlon (1924-1986): celebrated man of letters, known, among other things, for his selflessness and dedication to the loftiest moral values.

CONDEMNED

There is a void
Stuffed
With cotton-tenebrity;
Bequest for us; newborns
Treading the greed-scorched Earth

Death row
Is for souls that
Such rapacious times as these
Have tried
And found
Guilty
Of righteousness

Coffer entrails: staple delicacy for these budget*ivorous*
beings;
Long-handed executioners
Wheeling us; the damned
To our very end
Strapped
Helplessly
Unto gurney-days

May their *pavulon*
Become our elixir when reality alters its face
And the hand of inscrutability
Sugars
Into a sweet dream,
Each and every bitter nightmare

GROPING TIME

Mid day reveals me the world
But via the sight
Of closed eyes

Who pressed the sunlight switch
To plunge the land
This deep into night's own noon?

For what charcoal sin
Do we deserve
To be vouchsafed no more
Those cream-white nights
When the world did drift
Into an orgasm of slumber
At the moon's voiceless lullaby
And hearts still stood
As pristine
As Muanenguba's wilds of Lincoln green?

But now
A tenebrous suffering shrouds life's luminence
To groping time

BLACK OUT

Black out maroons me
Somewhere
In the middle of a nightmare
There
To reside
Amid sundry troubles with hideous faces

As immaculate white Paris
Admires with laughter – the woe in mosaic that hangs
On my walls smeared with mid night –

Hunger constipates me,
Laying me belly down
To crawl, python-like,
Over dust
Over mud

Then someday,
Listlessly, I shall stray
In the way
And make the day
Of lucky poachers
Returning from a fruitless hunt
For game like me

NIGHTMARE

In the nightmare of kings;
In crown-melting hell
There I dwell.

In a nightmare
From which princes awake
To say it was just a dream
There I live for real
My life
Of penury
Incarnated
In this leech

Stuck unto my right cheek;
This pain in mosses
Rooted in clusters to the bark of my soul

In a nightmare
I live
My true life
In a nightmare
From which kings and sultans awake
To say
It was just a dream

PSYCHOLOCAUST

Maggots squirm
In a mentality
Scavenged on
By cupidity-hyenas

Mice scuttle
On the floor
Of a thinking, littered
With the gnawed, shredded remnants
Of banknote stowaways

Eels of ill:
They swim-a-wriggle
In the reeking currents
Of blue blood

And in the world
Of reason
You and I get along

Very like Von Trotha and the Herero

MY NEIGHBOURHOOD

In my neighbourhood
They retreat crookedly ahead
And straight backwards
They advance

So therefore
In my neighbourhood
You must move ahead to the rear
At the front

In my neighbourhood
There are men whose hands
Hang down their left shoulders and vice versa
Just as if
The creator erred over them

And they eye you
Longing
In dead earnest
To dine
On your entrails

So therefore
You must walk crookedly ahead in my neighbourhood
Making sure
Your toes are facing
The direction whence you come

Ramshackle goings on

That once made – of my neighbourhood –
A shunned home
And of me,
A denigrated immigrant

In my neighbourhood
You couldn't stand it at all
The things your eyes should hear;
Not at all
The things your ears should see

So therefore
You'll do well to stick fingers in your nostrils
So as not to hear a word
In my neighbourhood
Do well to stick fingers in your ears
So as not to smell a thing

In my neighbourhood…

BENIGHTED

Spittle-wine in legislation-bottle, stoppered with deceit
I drink it at socio-economic gun point

Mistake not – for a squint in the hot sun –
My grimace of pain, O friend an ocean away!

See me here, in this artist's impression – unlike
An x-ray photo – of the bare-bodied:

No torso but a rib cage, in this
Skinning alive of pseudo-compatriots

To make drums of eerie rub-a-dubs
For the dance of vampires;

Perpetrators of the greed that starves me
To this skeleton in my country's cupboard.

And the dead dig graves in which to bury their living

BELIEF

I am a sufferer
Of pains
More excruciating
Than molten magma on the skin

So when karmic numbness
Shall deaden
The hand that clutches
That leash on the apocalypse of volcanoes,

On un-cringing feet
I shall be standing

I am a sufferer
Of hurts
More unbearable
Than the sudden chopping off
Of the finger as you slam the country's main door
Hard against our hand to the hinge

So when streaming tears
Shed from twenty million pairs of weeping eyes

Shall coalesce into a Genesian deluge,

On feet of belief
I shall be standing

And everywhere here
Is the affliction – with cancer of the mind –
Of those whom the devil
Anoints with his faeces

And on Sundays
A mud-reprobation
Stains each and every seeming white soul
Indelibly

LONGER THAN FOREVER

Droplet-nanoseconds:
They fall from hydro-time's firmament,
Watering the universe
Temporally

For ours
Is the gangrene
That caulks a land's core
Longer
Than forever

From a battered urn
Drink
Of my misery, liquefied

In mystery
And you'll suffer
Seven times over
The thirst of the Sahara

My genre of music
Is privation, sonor*ified*
To a cacophony for ears to bleed by

In the air
The addled-egg smack
Of malversational putrescence
Lasting
Longer
Than forever

OF GILDED THINGS, MISPLACED

Like refuse I am,
Dumped here...
In the abjectest part
Of indigence-streeted K-town

Only the eye
In the chilliest face
Of motley-headed penury looks my way
Everyday...
Every decade
Of every age

Imagine the pain, the blood
Of manliness from an injury so grave
When the most sordid, most jagged edge

Of many-sided poverty severs off the groins
Of the virile

So won't you be
So obliging – O surfeited brother, most affluent sir –
As to rush me to hospital this very minute,
Or must you be
Unfailingly
On your way to your adopted home of a hexagon?

Take me for a drivelling
Mendicant of a compatriot, for all I care,
But along the logical cracks in this parched wilderness
Tears of ink must flow
Scouring this vast dearth of rationale,
Unearthing bond fragments long buried
And gilded things, misplaced

IN A WRETCH'S EYES

This privation
Is armed with a gun from the arsenal of woe
Pointing at me
And a gravitational pull;

Frozen, all must drift perforce
To the iron-magnet, sizzling
With infernal hardship;
Anyone who dares to budge,
Bringing a hand to his pockets for a dime,
Is shot to misery

The beast's *koboko* tail

Flails me gnarled on the scrotum
Imagine sir!

Karmic despot decrees
That an entire day
Be dispensed with nought but a cocoyam to roast
In the noon sun

Better off deprived
Of the right, than be emptied thus
Of the verve – to vote

Night and day I fast
Not for piety's sake
But in subordination like suction
To the will-whirls of penury, done
On my earth
As it is
In the land beyond the beyond
Of nightmares

BEAUTIFUL SHIP

Wherefore are you bound, beautiful ship!
Sailing
So many knots away
Against the tides
Of stormy, smelly seas like these?

Won't you be lost, O beautiful ship!
In stormy, smelly seas like these
Taking the western way;
That perilous course

Away
From your destination's bay?

Wherefore are you bound, beautiful ship!
With sails of green, red and yellow
Going so many receding knots away
Over the murky, monster-ridden waters
Of stormy, smelly seas like these?

With rotted helm in cannibals' clutches
You sail on
Against the tides
Of stormy, smelly seas like these.

Tell me, O! Beautiful ship,
How many million league's more from here –
In these rainy nights and days –
Is anchorage?

MAGGOT PEOPLE

Look, O priviledged eyes, here
Where I reside
Opposite fiction's creepy places

Can't you see, O azure eyes, me;
This endangered specie
With habitat here, right here
Where red-hot surfeit flows, lava-like
Greed-scorching the earth?

In what millennium, O! Time to come, shall I be
A survivor

Of the ego-holocaust;
Escapee from this Auschwitz of grab
And swallow

And your lungs quaver
With syphilis night and day
As I drink
From your cornucopia of rheum
Coughed out of infected sore throats

My body lotion – as you know – is
A mixture
Of pus from your strangulated hernia
Incised
By the stiletto sun

And slime from your children's running noses,
Still I rub my glazed face with it as
I carry on my south bound shuffle
This,
To keep me moving in unrighteous paths

Look, O! affluent eyes, my way
Where you reside in me
Like maggots in the carcass of a lion

HEADLINES

A thousand days sleep and wake
On *Massive Fraud Uncovered...*
Issue after issue

Malversational drudgery

Wears out the sight of eyes
That seek to read about fatherland

In the chiefdom of a rodent reign
Gnawed letters of the alphabet
Produce shameful sounds
For a monotone of pilferage

The country's surname, soiled
By ink-phlegm spat on precious paper

I am done with headlines

MAMA'S GARDEN

Sap of quinine sweetness
The toxic flower buds hold:

Nectar of misappropriation

Mama's garden overgrows
With carnations of ginseng selfishness

Roses are black that emit
The sweet fragrance pernicious to lungs of the world

And swindle is alluring
With its intrinsic scent extracts from mints if the legal
tender

I wilt while bright-petaled hibiscuses of pilferage
Bloom in the global-warming sun

Tell me what flowers blossomed in Gethsemane
The day that thing which they say
Had been lost through disobedience
Was found?

THIS JESUS

Forty years in a wilderness
Which an aridif*ying* pilferage
Has made
Of a land of cornucopia

And a bottomless pit of temptation
In which to fall,
Taking with him
His Nazareth of compatriots

Messiah only
Of ethnocrats, this Jesus damns instead.
Power is his John the Baptist,
Not worthy
Of his wielding

As we dine
On a supper
Of rust from the rain and the wind on iron days,

This Jesus turns power into bread
And with his disciples
Eat to their fill,
Washing it down
With urnfuls
Of vinified saprophytism

And whenever he thirsts, crucifying us
This Jesus drinks, in seven gulps,
All of the Jordan

EREBUS

Cupidity-sepsis in ulcerous thoughts
Done…
Is the carnal rot of minds

In this tenebrity
Reserved for monstrosities
Comes a petrifying thing
As when a malversational epidemic
Decimates right down to the unborn

Two tear drops I shed
For a sun-shunned motherland:
The one for us; children of the shrouded noontide;
The other for them; senior scavengers in these
Predacious wilds of ethnocratic catabasis

Blood-like,
A third tear clots
Hard in the pupil

Who gives me eyes like August skies
Then I will cry the rains that rinse?

DISPENSATION

Out of our fair share
Of the smoked prawn,
Crapulent hearts stint us to ribs

Carrion in mangy bits, flung from
The marble verandahs of mansions,
At us; beasts of no nation whom karma
Has gyved to the rock of penury

Where the Good Samaritan!
To euthanatize me away
From this Erebian anvil, whereupon
Rapacious smiths malleate the mind
Into an arrowhead of despair?

Under skies of green, red and yellow
So it goes…
My woe

BRAVE NEW WORLD

I am a famish-eyed fledgeling, hatched
Among hibiscuses emptied of nectar;
That cleavage between my mother's buttocks
Where a lather of soap lingers
After she takes her hurried, childish shower

I am he who waited decades in the sun
Coming of age
To drink

At the source where waterflukes
Stick their suckers forever; this bare
Dried-out channel where only a few sunsets ago
A river gently flowed; that part
Of my mother's naked body
Which water never touches
Whenever she takes her careless, childish shower

I am he who has been
In that pack
Of migratory birds on a one-way flight
Fleeing the black rainy seasons of home
To nest in other foliages thinner than the mahogany's;
That part of my mother's naked body
Where the sponge never reaches
Whenever she takes her hurried, childish shower

And if, by any chance,
You see a tender petal
Of the flower of Mary
Crushed underfoot
And bleeding
Under the greedy tread
Of country wayfarers gone blind,
Then you've found me
Inside a brave new world

DEAD END
(Hinterland)

Wooden shack…
Smoke rises…
And lying scantily – in a battered, cupped aluminium

Shunned by disposal – are twenty or so seeds of beans
Boiled in salt...
Breakfast

At lunchtime
Sulking dancers move in time
To the rumbling music of famished bowels, carved
grimaces
On sun-dried concrete faces.
And how can misery-hardened cheeks
Ever hold a smile to you?

Come dusk, when seven or eight locust abdomens
Shall roast in the dying embers
Of decaying coconut peelings,
It shall be suppertime again;
Suppertime for them; lean beneficiaries
Of a usurped bequest; the rib-caged inheritors
Of a pilfered legacy

CITY OF LONGINGS

In the streets
My head splits from
The ventriloquist noon's mimicry –
In quadruple-pitch monotone –
Of cars, machines, birds and man

Underfoot, the market road
Vibrates to the sonorous, grains-of-sand numberlessness
Of human cackling in greed

Ceaseless travails

Still there is time
To watch the city's council
Bring down brick walls on hens and chicks,
Blessing them and saying *Amen*

Then suddenly, I realize
How hard it is
For the physical hand
To wipe off sweat in the soul

And I stand here
Dying
Of a mortal longing
For Muanenguba's evenings
When the dusk
Places a gag on the noise-lipped mouth of noon
Sitting captive amid coffee plants,
And awaiting freedom at the morrow's wrinkling
Of the dawn

COMMERCIAL ON ROTLAND

Once at your best
Of summer holiday destinations
Take a deep breath and
Relax in the swindle-fouled air of Rotland

Sup alfresco
On a dish
Of fish, dead
In lakes turned black from this
Massive spill of cupidity like an oil slick

Sit
On silted kleptomania
At rust-coloured river banks

And watch
Such natural phenomena
As money
Passing furtively
From one leprous hand
To the other
Etc...

Summer suns
And a pottage
Of sweet potatoes, blighted
In the ego-acidic content
Of Rotland's humus

There
Where such terrible marvels await you
Is Rotland;
Your land
Of promise

RECIPE

Pour a glass of skimmed graft in a pot
Set pot on hellfire and then
Put eight kilos of sun-dried STDs,
Two spoonfuls of the malaria spice
And a pinch
Of crushed penury.
Add half a litre

Of yellow water
Fetched in Douala, and
Leave to simmer for three generations and seven
minutes
Then put a handful
Of chopped malversation and
Stir for a hundred years and twelve seconds.
Add two lumps of rapacity-scented Anglophobia and
Leave to boil in privation for
Ninety-four decades three minutes and then
Serve hot

N.B For optimum savouring at table
Meal must be served
Alongside a drink
Of boiled headache in an earthen cup

DOUALA

The mist of travail
Hazes over January dawns
Souls in silhouette hit the road
In the early-morning rush
To slavish places of jobsites

Then one o'clock…!
Afternoons drenched in sweat;
Time for the usual scuffle with sultriness
When men hopelessly kick the air,
Suspended in the smothering hold
Of the vexed sun

In Bonaberi, at the foot

Of a Himalayan dump — where a woman in red
headscarf
Squats in a quickie of urinary relief —
A ragged urchin ferrets for lunch

Afflictions come to a head for these
Leech-infested siblings of mine; accursed sons
Of a gelded soil; these thousand and one faces
Uniformed in the fabric of glum looks;
These countless gaits
Held in place to a shamble
By the gravitational pull of privation

And hunger connives
With solar anger to make the famished mistake
A slender mirage on the road
For a serpent across the tarmac

PAIN

Another moon dies
As they say
No pay.
Seated by her three-stone fireplace
A needle-like housewife and her broomstick issues
Await the simmering little pot —
Of scanty maize grains and weevil — to cook

See what abjectness
Is reflected in the waters
Of this river
Taking its rise
From my eyes,

Coursing down my ugly face of stone
To the corners of my parched mouth

Yet five more moons have died
As they would say
Still no way
Hands with palms of concrete
Making money for ethnocratic mouths to devour

See what enslavement
Is reflected in the waters
Of this stream that takes it rise
From my brows
Coursing down my hideous face of stone
To the corners of my parched mouth
There, where trickles merge

How many decades more
To live to drink from this confluence of tears and sweat,
Salt to salt
Or shall it stay thus
Till dust comes to dust?

DRAB MONDAYS

I note these drab Mondays going by lately;
The privation-skinned race of days;
The boundary days between arid and horrid times
And in the dried-up palms of the hands of
These redundant brothers, wilting away in the
privatisation sun,
I see, reflected
Like things in a mirror,

Glazed eyes staring at me from the mists of unlived years
And as for me, I trudge on
Eastward of another drab Monday, unable
To figure out, quite unlike before,
Just how to quell
This mounting riot
Of famished entrails

THEIR EXCELLENCIES

Leprous captains at ship's helm,
Them; croupier-hearted misers,
They man the controls

And my cousin Andrew, he works
Under them; leprous captains at ship's helm
Pulling out, for less than a quarter a day,
Weeds or iron
Rooted in concrete

There is a senescent radio at the side
Of my cranky bed, held together by scraps of wire
It managed to tell me
Early this morning
That the price of our kerosene
Has been flung atop the Everest
By the hands of them; leprous captains at ship's helm,
Them; croupier-hearted misers

So my siblings!
Tonight you and I
Shall collect our urine in a bowl
To use to fuel our *bush lamp*, lest we –

Ants in the desert – get lost in
This dark night that emanates
Straight from men's souls

Leprous captains at ship's helm,
Them; croupier-hearted misers,
They man the controls

AUTOPSY REPORT ON CONSTABLE MVONDO

White maggoty cluster;
Rot of the brain matter.
Bulge of stomach is protrusion that carries
A tangled ball of *ascaris*.
Entrails examination performed
Observation: too rot deformed
Reeking phlegmatic effusion
At incision of bulbous anal inflammation

Examiner's nasal sense
Besieged by a most foul whiff of the putrefaction
incense
Conclusion:
Cadavre in advanced state of long-throat consumption

Cause of death shares pathological affinities
With that of other parasite species.
For undue, superfluous sips from the bottled
perspiration of the just
Dracula fangs bite the dust

Yaws on the fingers that pilfered

And rot from the unuttered malediction of those who offered
Right hand carries gangrene traces
From frequent palm contact with the slime of highway squeezes

Entire autopsy team expresses profound wishes
May soul of deceased rest in perfect pieces

PEACE OF MINE

Walk, O Walker! For no mile at all
In my black pair of shoes, walk
To where I quench – with water
Fetched from pain wells – my ebony thirst;

Pain wells
Dug way down, past the mind's granite
To where a screech owl, caged within me
Beats wings against my fragile organs, its claws
Scratching the inside of my torso, going
To make, of blood,
My watery stool

And fouling, with sewage droppings
My blood stream and hormone rivulet, pecking
With ivory beak at my membranous heart and lungs,
Bursting open my filmy bladder
To bathe, as ducklings do,
In spilled, *un*-pissed urine
Collected in pools
Down in my insides

Its screeching
Becoming my speech
As I open my mouth to speak

Walk, O Walker! for no mile at all
In my black pair of shoes, walk
And you'll come to know
What ease and what peace
Is mine

Keep me but a moment's company, O Walker!
Sitting
In this centre of pain whirls, where a pied crow
Shall be trapped within you, darting in flights
About your insides, scratching
With every movement, balancing
With talon*ned* claws against the rib railing
Of its human cage dripping blood,
And bathing, as ducklings do
In your internal haemorrhage

Hopping and perching
Upon your guts to the spill of *un*-shat faeces,
Spattering
With flapping wings
That pre-waste of metabolic mud
All over your torso's inside, and pecking
With ivory beak
At germs and viruses that swim
In the tides of haemoglobin

Its crowing
Becoming your speech
As you open your mouth to speak

Keep me but a moment's company, O Walker!
Sitting
In this centre of pain swirls
And you'll come to know
What ease and what peace
Is mine

HIJACKED
(DON'T TELL ME)

Don't tell me
All you got from the Sorbonne
Is how stealthily
To take over
This commuter train aboard which
You and I were born;

Terrorists with kleptomanic intent

Don't tell me
That worsted know-how of yours
Is all great Harvard ever gave
For this slow-moving train to be hijacked;
Train that left Nineteen Sixty Station for Hazy Morrows;
Train aboard which
You and I were born

The longest handed of men I ever saw

Don't tell me
All there was to bring back home from Ife
Is but a big head, stuffed

With perversion enough to cause to derail
Into the swamp of deprivation – this train
Aboard which
You and I were born

Pick pocketing intelligentsia of the aeon

Don't tell me
All UNIYAO churns out
Is but a long-throated manner of men
To loot, amid the shrill cries of helpless passengers,
The rear wagon
Of this train aboard which
You and I were born

Don't tell me…

DEFINITION

To make anguish incendiary…

To live to char
in a fire
of which Hell
is but a simulacrum

To fabricate from tinder
your tribulation
so the flesh could roast
in flames of terracotta drabness

To live to burn
in an arson

of brown blazes
till you long
so fervently for a plunge
into the furred tides of the longest sleep;
the last slumber of men

To make anguish incendiary…

To fabricate from tinder
your tribulation…

is poverty

WORKING CLASS LOVERS

Dusky close of day
I retire home to cockroaches, to symphonies sung by
mosquitoes
And to a grass-soup supper,
Envious
Of the spent sun
Going to sleep
On cloud-fleece beddings of gold

Come tonight's twilight
When the pretty moon with cream-white smile
Seduces the dark-skinned night,
Two wraiths shall, once again
Fleet by into hell;
My better half and I

And how can your paper kerchiefs
Dry our tears; the shedding of which

Is in the heart?

MY DEATH

I live off putrescence
Crunching crisp-fried cankerworms

I scoop rot off the organs of my dead epoch
To season and devour

The baby is spoon-fed with gangrene
Scraped off its mother's festering mind.

Buried neck deep in the wilderness
They set my head afire

So, to the friend who seeks to know
What my death is made of,
I tell
Of the great grandmother of tribulations
And of evil
Greater
Than perdition can punish

Till the souls seeps ethereally
Through karmic walls of steel

THE DEFALCATION CRAZE

Who looks down with pity
At us; parch-mouthed souls
Here below

Waiting in vain
For the slaking rain
Licked dry in midair
Into the atmosphere tongue
Of esurience?

Who drinks
To consciences charred callous
In this one great blaze
Of incendiary greed?

And Quislings hasten the plunder rush
To a zillion miles an hour
As though
This life will end for sure
First thing tomorrow morning

II

NINETEEN BUGLE CALLS

INTERMENT

Remember that burial
Of the living;
How we all lay
Inside our hardened-dung sarcophagus
And that terrible platter
Of earth upon the lid
As the grave refilled?

Remember those faces
Clothed
In the fabrics of expression, somewhere
Between denim sadness and polyester leers
Looking down
At us; coffined scum?

Remember the chatter
Six feet above us, heard
Somewhere between distinctive jeers and mournful cries
Even as we lay there, somewhere
Between living death and death itself?

And government is a phoney loving husband
Always dressed
In that tattered suit of his shredded vows.
I am his dear wife's brittle heart
Lying
In vitreous shards

These grab-and-swallow days
Soaked in my tears;
Days that, like a million match flares,
Have shrivelled away from me

My faith in you reduced to latex

FANGS

The midday sun connives with
These penurious hours of red-eyed days
To scorch, with famine,
The tender stomachs of little ones

In the heat of seven-year terms
Toiling gravediggers watch their perspiration
Licked off their brows
By the crocodile tongues of dyed-haired, moustached
prodigals

And milk tears, shed
From suffering eyes:
They fall straight into the longest throats down below
Of black-suited gluttons

On the same spot
I take to my heels
Away from fangs that daunt the world
Breaking into a stampede
The glaze-eyed faithfuls of misery's creed

COME WHAT SUNDAY!

Come what Sunday
Shall I be brave enough
To cringe from
These exotic star-spangled cravings

That play havoc
On the fragile soul?

Come what Sunday
Shall I be courageous enough
To take to my heels at the sight
Of these sabre-edged desires
Wielded
From the hilt of finite things?

For as this stilleto*ed* mania –
Honed on the whetstone of materialist lure –
Hacks my thoughts to bits of sin,
Irresistibly I dip this last of my ten fingers
Into that grease of retch which lubricates
The rust-ridden engine
Of this ship of state

CONFESSIONS OF THE BULL

On this death road, plied
By battered hooves to the perdition of slaughter
Shuffle us; this hapless herd
Of a tailless cattle not just from the Adamawa
But out of the river of prawns.
Our *nganakoh* is Jean-Jacques from the Hexagon
While ticks on our bodies
Are our own kinsmen.
Imagine sir!

But these immaculate white egrets; avian incarnations
Of goodwill, this Earth's noble hearted, are our saviours
Though, I wished,

Of the soul

BLOOD BROTHER

How much redder, your majesty
Than that of anyone who dwells
Within this rotund ephemeris
Is the colour
Of your royal blood?

How much more majestically, your highness,
Than my slavish blood
Does it flow through veins?

And should these razor phrases
Go slitting your throat
How much less gory will be its spill
Than that of us; crumb-eating scum
Who dwell under your mighty feet?

Exclude me not from your genealogy, O! Blood brother,
When next you draw up your family tree
And when next you go communing
With your illustrious forebears
For benediction from the vast beyond

GOING FOR A WALK

Down the pilfering way, charted
By quislings of long-throatedness
To banks without a river;
To banks without a dime

Of silver

Through kleptomanic by-ways, charted
By hydrogen-bomb desires
Down to a water*less* shore

Here…
To quench –
With a glassful of Kalahari's dearth –
My pillage-wrought thirst

They that glut on the land's entrails
Only set the table
For a feast on their own children's children's brain matter
When the last becomes the first;
When the strange thing that goes around
Shall come around

SOIL

Showers of heavy urine-rains:
They percolate into thee; the season's watery sewage, disposed
From the bladders
Of his black-suited Excellencies

…and then
Croaking, green-limbed things
Hang down from the boughs; thy mango trees
Have fruited frogs, ripening
Into toads

O, for a solar quirk!
That the retributive sun
Might come and char this hideous congestion of freaky
noons
Off my heydays

But knowing
How vanity always colours – with a shade of illusion –
This and other fervent wishes,
Makes my soul bleed

RAGE

Out of reeking pig dung
My ballpoint pen erects a statue of you;
Out of exasperation

Out of stale dog retch
The hands of my words raise monuments in your
downtowns;
Out of despair

And through these journeying breezes
I send up to heaven
Tidings of your foulness
And, for all I care,
Ignominy is what I tell of you;
The stampede, the suicide and the greed
Over crumbs of salted caked faeces
Fed to the blind

If to each son of this desecrated soil
Is a tribute to pay,

I do mine this day
In vituperative lines
Written
In the ink of my watery stool

PAPA'S LAND

Disdain moves the feet that trample
On us; poor squatters on affluent grounds
Ill will moves the mouths which, calling us,
Chew our names to chaff

As if to say
The most hapless of this world's accursed
Is our only kindred: we; mendicants in papa's land

Yaws in their lungs from the greed-borne disease
That fills the heart with pus
And I wish to Lucifer
That I'd be dead in this dead of night, killed
By virtuous things

So let sweat from the soles of your feet
Moisten the dusty road as you tread barefooted
O! Famished emigrant, away from papa's land;
Fart-fouled, sin-soiled shrine where in our midst
Ignobly rests his soul;
Rocky place on which
My patriotism, glassier than yours,
Crashes to sunlit shards

DAMAGING DIRECTORS

Do not slaver but weep
At this culinary whiff from kitchen parastatals
As stewards of the enslaving republic
Grate me down to cocoyam paste
On grater-mandates seven years long
To make supper for their Excellencies: them; eaters
Of *mbongo tchobi*

Unlike the world under the sun, see me here,
Perishing
Under this duress called poverty
Born
Of the insatiety
Of centaur-kings

I live
Through K-Town nights, when
Darkness sings a dirge for us; the dying
In destitution, begotten
Of the trait-monster that governs the governor

And sunrise will not light up minds in the
Blackout of gulosity

Tell me! Will theirs not be
A retch of fire who surfeit, compelled
On this pork-tribulation?

PATRIOT

Days without noons under the pilfering rain
Drenched to my thoughts in the abjectness
Of a poverty even the church rat fears, scuttling
For cover in ailurophilic places

But in the nationalist sun I dry this conscience of mine,
wet
With precipitation from reeking skies

Now is time out to respire
Or we all expire
For fatality shall shun asphyxia when the breath
Holds out in lung-fortresses
Till noisome days go by in capitulation.

Miracle!

Who dreads vultures in this death
When decay flees my mortal remains in horror?

ADMONITION

Graft-motes
Carried
In wind-farts that blow my way

Whiffs of terribleness
Wafted
In nights of brown darkness, when
Dead rat and other stenches
Waylay the moral nostril

Inhale not, O! pen-peer, the lung-withering oxygen
To die
Of this cancer
Of the longthroat,
Bereaving the tribe
Of the patriot in you

ARISE!

In the skull and cross-bone days
Of parliamentary *draculocracy*,
When cranial-nuts
Crack open under the hammer of surfeit – and sucked
To political obesity, is the people's brain matter;
Swine fodder for them; hogs of men –
Lost
Is battle not fought
Back to back with fellows

So up from slumber, O countryman of letters!
And pick up your spear of jagged diction, penned
From infuriated biros,
To face the gastrocrats
And, hard in the eye,
Stab them one and all

THE MOTTO

What peace…
In this war with privation's infantry battalion
When hunger-bombs fall in trench bowels?

No retreat

What work…
Here, where I've had as much *honour most respectfully*…
As to deplete the ink in a million biros,
Numbing to paralysis
The hand that writes it?

No surrender

What fatherland…
Wherein shoeless compatriots
Bleed on the sole, walking
On thorn-tarred ways?

Carry on
Is all there is to do
In this power mockery from
The leer of faces on state television,

When scoffing voices from
The national radio news
Taunt you to the soul

Carry on, soldier! my heart tells me
For true doers live athwart the jeers and cheers
Of spectator minds

WASTE OF A JAZZ BAND

This slavery throws thick rust on percussion instruments
Cushioning to muteness
The jar of cymbals

From underneath the pianist's fingernails
Secretions of incendiary evil set keyboard afire

Raptor of a winged dumbness lands on the throat
Plucks off singer's voice.

No ears fetch supple strains from velvety voices
To quench the musical thirst
Of love-struck hearts

With what…
To pluck musical strings
When the guitarist's fingers
Go to fill the stomach
Of famished leprosy?

Player's bad breath and spittle
Degenerate the trombone to a cranky disuse

As microphone *un*-sings – in retching mode – lyrics that
Into it the devil had sung,
Help tidy up, dear cleaner bard
This squalid stand, littered
With the wire and plywood wreckage
To which state musicians
Have vandalized the cello

COUNSEL

Decades on end in stampedes of grab
My chagrin is hued in olive drab

Fingers and fingers linger still in the till
Wonder not, then, how even the soul manages to take ill

Amid a clangourous inferno of hustle and bustle
Mine are the woes that chink and rustle

But if – this vortex of transience – your conscience does
withstand
Before God and man, in Etheris you shall stand

INFANT PRODIGY

Sulks, sobs and cries…
Running nose over greasy rags,
Scratching and picking at your
Measle*d* little buttocks.
Who bereft you thus
Of your parentage?

Those lines I see running down your cheeks
I recognize;
They are the tracks of your tears.

So close, so next of kin
Are you and I
That I can tell
When and how you turned orphan,
The sad and wry story

Of your puny life;
The very chapters where your biography
Makes for a ribald read

Infant prodigy,
Abandoned;
Dumped into the rot of retrogression
Like foetus
Disposed of
In a latrine.
How the rodents have nibbled away
At your prodigiousness!

Do you hear my sobs too, O infant prodigy!
From there where you stand amid those ruins
Of a dilapidating legacy;
Your hard-earned ancestral bequest?

Whatever changes
Have made or marred these youngish days of yours,
Deep in the bowels of old mother *Wouri,**
Lie unaltered records of your christening
Like a chested treasure
Underneath everlasting meanders

*River from which Cameroon got its christening

HINDSIGHT ON TOMORROW
MY PEOPLE!

On a million and one belying faces
Could be seen
The surface of woes
Smeared
With laughter

Then
Weird dreams – shunning sleep to stick to my
wakefulness –
Of hunter soldiers
Crossing the Mfoundi
To the lair on the seventh hill
There
To muffle a lion's roars

And the wild was rid
At long last
Of its dread-predation

INTERMENT II

Today
The end of days
Of national mourning in a palm grove:
No more keening at the riverside:
Us; moaning suppliants at the foot
Of freedom liquefied to a tidal flow

Today

I offer my ballpoint pen as catafalque
For that sarcophagus of defalcation wherein lies
A nation; the governors that purloined from me
My happiness

Make this dark ink
To flow six-foot deep, O god of poetesses!

Make us; hoodooed ones, the most deserving
Of a funeral